VIEW
FROM
TRUE
NORTH

Crab Orchard Series in Poetry

Open Competition Award

VIEW
FROM
TRUE
NORTH

poems by

Sara Henning

Crab Orchard Review &
Southern Illinois University Press
Carbondale

Southern Illinois University Press
www.siupress.com

21 20 19 18   4 3 2 1

The Crab Orchard Series in Poetry is a joint publishing venture of
Southern Illinois University Press and *Crab Orchard Review*. This
series has been made possible by the generous support of the Office
of the President of Southern Illinois University and the Office of
the Vice Chancellor for Academic Affairs and Provost at Southern
Illinois University Carbondale.

Editor of the Crab Orchard Series in Poetry: Jon Tribble
Judge for the 2017 Open Competition Award: Adrian Matejka

Cover illustration: "Female Torso in White Marble," by
Theanthrope, cropped. iStock

Library of Congress Cataloging-in-Publication Data
Names: Henning, Sara, author.
Title: View from true north : poems / by Sara Henning.
Description: Carbondale : Crab Orchard Review & Southern
Illinois University Press, [2018] | Series: Crab Orchard Series
in Poetry
Identifiers: LCCN 2018011505 | ISBN 9780809336852 (paperback)
| ISBN 9780809336869 (e-book)
Subjects: | BISAC: poetry / American / General.
Classification: LCC PS3608.E564536 A6 2018
| DDC 811/.6—dc23
LC record available at https://lccn.loc.gov/2018011505

Printed on recycled paper ♻

This paper meets the requirements of ANSI/NISO Z39.48-1992
(Permanence of Paper). ∞

For Matthew

CONTENTS

VIEW
FROM
TRUE
NORTH

FIRST MURMURATION

When I say a son
        broken open by his father

is becoming a starling,
        I mean feathers are unfurling
from his skin, and confused

as he is by his wrists
        uncoiling, by his thumbs

angling into a dirt
        -flushed twosome of bastard
alulae, he imagines

he's only a boy
        unhitching the day

from his shoulders,
        boy rushing through a whole
fruit orchard of minor

grievances, the sun
        -bruised flesh of the fallen

scenting the backs
        of his knees. When I say
a son broken open

by his father, I mean
        a son, not a sweat-split Eden

where *no* only means
        he's rising through fog,
not a sheen of danger,

a canopy of trees
        silking the soles of his

pollen-luscious feet.
        When I say a son broken
open, I mean

a son shape-shifting
        past the velvet scrim

of orchard and ether,
        a son who learns
to leave his body

at the first slow pierce
        of his father's song.

I

CAMERA LUCIDA

> *I was there. I know.*
> —C. D. Wright, *Deepstep Come Shining*

Let me be witness, Lord,
not half-silvered mirror.

Let me know heirloom
from hazard, my name

from a legacy of hyssop
so filial my arms

tangle in sharp calyxes,
my heart confuses petals

for bruise. Suffer me
until shame is my only

angle of incidence. Let my
truth, graceless squall

that it is, hold you like
a lover. Instead of words,

watch shadows graffiti
my skin and ripen. Lay

your hands on my beautiful
braille. If you cannot

deliver me, forgive me
my trespass. The discreet

side of revelation still
calls me home.

RITES OF PASSAGE: A CONDITIONAL

Whitefish Bay, Wisconsin, 1966

If my mother slips into a canopy of leaves to watch apples,
their slurred geographies of bruise and inflorescence, pelt
the soil below her. If it's the hour when Dean Martin gushes
through living room windows, when curtains exhale with his
voice's smoky pulse. If the Big Brass hour pendulums between
fixity and ground zero—*You're nobody 'til somebody loves you.*
If her father's voice fuses to the lilt, fourth martini—*You're
nobody 'til somebody cares.* If she rips her brother from fantasy
raids, his G.I. Joes febrile with hands or heat. If sister on her hip,
they sprint through familiar incarnations of breaking glass,
listening for their mother's sharp exhale as her body hits the wall.
If they hush their way upstairs into closets, haunt the metal
underside of beds. If cotton and leather swathe their bodies.
If they remember their coordinates, silk pressed to their faces:
Always a different location. A game of memory. If bedroom
crawl space, then bathroom cabinet: wherever their bodies,
contorted into shapes of fear and corduroy, can slink. If she tells
them: *Breathe lightly.* If she says *gather your breath into a small
orb of light and hold it in your chest.* If children, still as lamps,
silhouette themselves with curtains, know they've entered
a game of waiting: *Hold it there. Try not to let go.* If the needle
grafts the record's face, if her mother's voice hazards a smoke
-sieged saxophone solo. If the same fluid mornings, sensual
with chill, still wound the air, or if dead leaves curl like burning
ends of cigarette paper: *Leave them.* If shouts, metallic
and lean as the rake-shaped marks on a child's legs, still
linger. If a hurt turns luscious and stark as a son muscled open,
if the family cat zigzags down memories now instead
of hallways, will she remember his moans? If years later,
a mother still steels herself with brandy and reruns
of Lawrence Welk, will her daughter forgive her? If half
-washed dishes still glide in a roil of suds, if cocktail glasses

fool the kitchen with their glistening, will they blaze
through the float of jazz? Tell me, if they burn themselves
luminous—the dishes, the daughter, the years forsaking
them—will they form a halo big as the moon?

HOW I LEARNED I HAD THE SHINE

1988

For days, when asphalt
        seethes through the still-wet
            scrapes, I'm shacked up

            in the deep-freeze box
        my grandfather resurrects
from the dump. I bastion

and sulk there, shunning
        my grandmother's hand-me-
            down pumps and floral

            jacquard, throw pillows
        masking cardboard ragged
as my ponytail. So let's begin

with the Huffy scooter,
        my jelly sandals glittering
            between escape

            velocities. The gutter
        water I fishtailed through
while grinding curbs,

skirt splitting at the kick
        pleat, blood perfuming
            the air. Now, instead

            of watching my grandfather
        razor windows he'll dress
with valances, lathe

saloon doors from closing
      flaps, I'm lifting the gauze,
            feeling for rocks shape-

            shifting under the crystalline
      scabs. I'm making bets
with myself on which will

purge the surface, petite
      rosettes, and which will
            loiter, tacit and pure,

            in my skin. The lapsed
      grit I'll learn to smooth
my hands over, hard

as my grandfather's rage
      when his martini lunch
            cuts through modesty,

            and my mother urges us
      toward the amnesty of our
rust-stung Chevrolet.

Vermouth's nude
      currency flits through
            his glass now, but I've

            given myself to clairvoyance,
      the highballs and tinctures
of Dubonnet that will

suture the afternoon,
      his eyes like sow thistle
            as my mother guns

the engine. I'm watching
the slice of lime strong-
holding the rim

lose its clutch, too
thick and planchette-
shaped not to yearn

for baptism, *dirty girl,*
broken hyoid, slinking,
not vortexing, down.

FOR MY UNCLE, WHO LEARNED TO FLY

> *Their sons grow suicidally beautiful*
> *At the beginning of October*
> —James Wright, "Autumn Begins in Martins Ferry, Ohio"

On nights moths cyclone and plunge
      into my car's low beams, I'm convinced
            they are bodies in love—forewings ricochet
      against parabolic reflectors

in cadence, thoraxes pelt the cool
      tease of glass. Because spring thaw
            suffers them into the crosswind's whirl,
      the dirge of the suicidally beautiful

becomes a rousing bell. When I learn
      that celestial routing plots their spiral
            flight paths, not longing, that my light's heady
      ploy is another logic

betraying me, I think of my uncle,
      knees down in wildflowers, the day
            my mother broke his arm. I imagine the clash
      over a blue ukulele,

his ulna split by its cheap wood,
      the way the nylon strings feathered
            his skin. I want to touch his cast's exhausted
      foxhole as he secrets

his pain inside of it, to arch
      into its raw cotton. I want to close
            my eyes over nights their father forced them
      into the cellar, spurred him

onto his sister with joint locks
>and vital point strikes *to teach her*
>>*a lesson*, his body thrust forward by their
>father's slurs. Years later,

grinding his thighs into boot
>-marked bleachers at the rodeo, my uncle
>>watches cowboys launch toward steer bolting
>from spring-loaded chutes,

watches for hands full of horns,
>man given over to adrenaline and dust.
>>He gazes as man seizes beast like a child
>held between another

child's hands. Before my uncle
>leaves for boot camp, he'll hold his sister's
>>wrist until she vines her fingers around his thumb
>sequined with nicotine

stains. It is the last time
>his hands will plot her vein's smooth
>>tributaries, trail the map of scars to her pulse.
>Next autumn, a bullet

will sing its way into his skin.
>But for now, like honeysuckle
>>twisting hard at the root it loves or betrays,
>she won't let go.

MARILYN

She's a bivouac stitched into marquisette, not a schooner gleaming over a siege of water.

She's looking hard at her hips jettisoned in fabric, her eyes glassy as a cat's, looking hard for the serenade—*Happy Birthday, Mr. President*—still surging its forgone gift between her tongue and glottal. Instead, she finds a tarantella of subway air quivering at her thighs. It's not sultry, this trompe l'oeil of bone sweltering under bone.

Once my mother locked me in the bathroom with her, swallowed a whole bottle of quaaludes. When my grandmother picked the lock with a paper clip, she found me on the plush carpet next to her, pretending to dream.

I could have been staring into my mother's face, murmuring *siege*, then *sunder*. I could have been pretending my father had not killed himself the week before. Instead, I'm fantasizing about a black hole nesting, invisible and insatiable, in the center of the Milky Way.

In Kansas, years later, scientists would claim they could create a black hole that would propel a spaceship. First, square kilometers of solar panels plaited into the cosmos like a field of glass heather, gamma ray laser pointed and waiting for the spherical shell of photons to bloom.

And then a hole, not the renegade daughter who, after years of extradition, still supernovas for no one. And then a girl, not the hole vibrating on its spin axis that's foraging for pulsars, purging radiation into space's dusky tapestry.

Instead of the next phase of human destiny, I'm thinking of Marilyn's face, frantic and sainted, in the white telephone's gloss. I'm thinking of the light thawing around her body, so pearlescent the morning they found her.

Marilyn, facedown on her duvet. Marilyn, every effigy of bone or joint tangled, not shattered, in its own discretion of vertigo. Nothing in her moon-kissed shoulders, the supple compliancy of sheen and freckle, would save her.

I'm thinking of the bathroom's wall sconces bathing my mother's nearly breathless body with light.

I believe she will wake up thinking *anything can be gripped into darkness*.

I believe I'll open my eyes and see the ship upbraiding the sky.

FOR MY SISTER, MISCARRIED

> *Something else*
> *Hauls me through air—*
> —Sylvia Plath, "Ariel"

Fluxing through the last
      known tor of lineages, she's
         a cellular schism,

         not an arrow, just one
      ectopic hymn quickening
from my mother's other

mouth. I'm three,
      watching my mother
         thumb her body not

         for traces of my father,
      suicidal clusters of myogenesis,
but for a sign—my birth

the first thrown
      insurgence, silky nectar
         scraped from the petal.

         My sister is feral hydrangea
      rioting all summer, another
bastard daughter

rotting the family vine.
      Every known savior crests
         from a woman's body—

         her body a combine
      threshing chaff from straw.
I watch my mother

bind what's left
     of my sister in the skirt
          haloing her ankles, burn

        her like musk
     thistle culled from my father's
grave. I wait for the hole,

the blaze. For hours,
     we choke on cinder,
          salt, envy the only

          cauldron-bound spirit
     among us to quit her
mother's body, fly.

OTHER PLANETS, OTHER STARS

At the shooting range, my mother and aunt
      single out pistols, set aside an hour to palm
the grip of unversed steel, trigger guard,

      every barrel's delicately latticed gorge.
And after, they inundate targets at their chakra points,
      first head, then heart. Flare after flare

penetrating paper. Astronomers say that only one in five
      stars like the sun hosts an earth-sized world,
but I can't stop thinking of the smaller planets,

      gaunt and mysterious, little martyrs of rock
accelerating in circuit, wondering what's to come.
      I'm quarantined in the lobby, a pair of muffs

sheathing my ears. I'm not old enough to fear
      men who swagger through unlocked doors, to slip
a hand under the bed skirt night after night

      like my mother every time our house moans
under a broken stud, discerning metal from ruche.
      Not every world has the girth to sashay

against gravity, so it hoards what it can. Planets
      pulverized to radiant dust become girls of panic
and stone. I watch through bulletproof glass

      how my mother now mimes the length
of the pull, metal jacketing the bullet's scorching interior.
      I want to be a planet far from this

sisterhood of Kepler data, where silhouettes
       of men exert strong centrifugal force. I want
to be a soft glint of rock heralding her own

       inertia, body without magnetic field
distorted by another celestial urging—aim the muzzle
       like a solar tsunami. Detonate or run.

THE ART OF DROWNING

When her best friend feigned
her own drowning, her body

sinking as if ransomed by
water, my ten-year-old

mother dove after the luster
of bathing suit breaching

a tide too ready to swallow her,
blonde hair sleek as a jellyfish

pulsing in flotsam and milky
lacquer. The girl's laugh

a cleaving oyster.
My mother still under her,

spitting up shame and spume.
Every unburied delta

that moved through her body
became a torrent

disgracing her starboard.
Years later, every lover exploiting

her water's lush vertigo
a lesson in spindrifts, sternways,

shells that sliver her toes.
Because I'm trickster,

heiress of disaster,
I'll learn to hold my breath

until I'm grit and glisten,
cull and foam. Until

like my mother, I confuse
love for mooring, not gravity's

tideward fidelity, not one
more ruthless pull.

MY LIFE IN MEN

Summer Enrichment Camp, 1989: Discover Asia!

<blockquote>

yes,
I am here, these are my borders, hold me down
a little while. Make me real to myself.
—Lynda Hull, "The Window"

</blockquote>

I can't stop wanting his Wranglers
and dirty Reeboks, his haunting lilt

of duplexes and airbrushed angels,
so I'm easing my thumbs through

a fortune cookie's curling perimeters,
because I'm after the paper heart

I'll stow in my hip pocket until I reach
him, the other scholarship kid,

my solo coterie of the less-blessed,
because his Henley rolled to the elbows,

his razored-in-the-kitchen crew cut
is a dialect still wooing me: in it,

my mother holding my chin under
fly-thick fluorescent light, my bangs

between her fingers as my aunts ash
their menthols, man-hating thick

as the smoke haloing us. I want
to drop the fortune on his desk

like I'm testing the crystal-skinned
crescents of har gow I pinch

and steam until they resemble
the skin on the other girls' hands,

smooth as pashmina, heat splicing
like shrimp luscious in the core.

The pink, like their nails, indecently
radiant. Dressing for our Kabuki

recital, I tighten my obi, fantasizing
that it's his hands, cuticles ruthless

with engine oil, wrapping me in their
muscular silk. While our teacher

poses us, I caress the slips of my fan
lacquered with cherry blossoms,

while he's all samurai, knees splayed
and lunging. And that's why desire

and disgrace are the same pantomime—
his solo Kami Mai rash among

Styrofoam stage dragons and smirking
Buddhas, witch hazel stinging

my eyes as I scrub rice powder
from my face. The fortune like an eel

lithe and untamable, he unfolds,
then lingers over—the girls he'll knock

up, meth that will age him into
a wizened child warrior, I read

in his body, his fingers on my wrist
now, his touch its electric tail.

SONG

1970

The song of my mother / punching her father / in the heart is not

≪⑤

The song of her feet / all grime and spent sneakers / kicking up hallelujahs

≪⑤

Is not the song of her shins / the surge and flush / of everyday bruises

≪⑤

I mean the song / like the animal's cage she's breaching now / is past salvation

≪⑤

I mean the song / the hamster or the girl's soft scatting / through glitz and
    splinter

≪⑤

Is a song of glass / a slow song drowning the afternoon / in dulcet, blue notes

≪⑤

The kind a father sings / while forcing his daughter's body / to the floor

≪⑤

The kind that swells from a daughter's hands / lovely and graceless / so that
    when

≪⑤

She punches him once, twice / this song of thrumming / overwhelms the air

᪥

Can you hear it? / The song *acutest at its vanishing*? / Her father's heart?

᪥

Her body's brute arpeggio? / Is it a song of erasure gone wrong? / Do you call it

᪥

Bone of my bones / *Flesh of my flesh* / A fist-shaped longing chiseled out of light?

CONCORDANCE FOR MY GRANDFATHER'S DEMENTIA

He no longer remembers her name,
so my mother buys my grandmother
a rooster. He falls off his chair, so
my mother triages each of his threats—
ambush of fists, elbows gaunt through
leathered skin. She holds him on his knees,
grits these words through her teeth: *you'll never
hit me again.* He's the feral cock lying
in a throng of dandelions, their fierce heads
gone to seed, the last summer I camouflaged
myself in fields instead of some boy's
arms. Fox piss, tail feathers, a geography
of organs lashed into countries—no
heuristic for this whole bruised longitude
of animal. I dressed his wounds, crushed
aspirin into water when his shrieks
skinned the wind clean. I named him
for how the rasp of the dying lurked
in his crow, iron murmured into sugar—
True Shepherd. I named him for how
his comb throbbed with each squawk, lusty
as souls no longer forsaken. *True Shepherd,*
not the bird still nameless we will bury
in a grocery sack. Not my grandfather's
final fall. Not his body interned in pewter,
not his cache set aside to scatter. Not even
the animal maimed in the sward. *True
Shepherd*—beautiful bastard—whom the sun
never answered, no matter how lushly
he called.

DRUNK AGAIN, HE PUSHES HER

If she falls this time, my grandmother,
into the cluster of cacti she nursed from

blunt-cut pups, if she awaits her wounds
to callous like lobes nicked to stomata,

or spines scarring their way into woolen
areoles, she'll laugh until the sultry lure

of shame is beyond her. If the golden barrel
stems stake her flesh this time, purloining

through breach and bract, if they take
hours to pluck while flowers genuflect

from the crown of globes cresting loose
from pot to linoleum, spilling dirt in which

she's learned to rest her head, she'll coax
each deep-clenched thorn refusing closure

with her nails, its pulpy, fevered *now*.
If the woman-pain threading through the yard,

up the stairs, to the place she's fallen does
so by instinct now, the way that untamed,

it's learned to lay its body upon her, she'll use
the word *accident*, blame her German

shepherd's sweet-sly heft. And if somewhere
she's still falling, half-erect, half-floating,

if the alibi she learns to mouth is quilled
into her blood like a siren song, I'll say *this*

is how I'm falling, this is how I fell—gravity
my heirloom, my bluntly conjured flare.

RAIN ELEGY

Korsakoff's syndrome, 2009

July and my grandfather
sentries the garage, watching

for the unchained repetition
of water. He's fluent

in monsoon trough, jet streams,
every convergence zone

flashing on the Weather
Channel at the top of the hour.

He shifts to the window,
expecting the sky's dry burn

to perjure its oath not to wail
and dirge, to release its blue,

humid and irreverent as the sweat
-shirt he's worn every day

since March, his brain hostile
to encoding the seasonal turn.

He waits for rain like the rapture,
like he waits for his wife's

poached eggs on Sunday, so raw
and supple they radiate shamelessly

into the buttered rinds of toast,
his brain like the yolk's molten

seams. His memories untether
into these tarns of silk, lush

as they elide and harden. Every
day of this drought he waits,

won't leave the television to eat,
to steep his ripe clothes in

the washing machine, for the sun
-breached flood might unleash

its grief to another man's ether,
might split the sky with a water

too brutal and strange to suffer
its way anywhere but home.

BAPTIZE HIM IN DARK WATER

I.

Blackout, 1990

My grandfather's neurons are ferrying the story
of his body across dark water. But let's begin
with citronella candles, mosquitoes haunting his bled
martini glass. Jags of heat-whelmed ice too sultry

not to thieve through the specular reflection
spiral into a raid of light. I want to tell you
about the back deck takeout, honeysuckle draping
the wood lap siding. Sesame chicken

exit-wounding from his mouth unswallowed,
slicking his linen shirt. I want to tell
you about his body going fetal, my egg roll

glinting in its oil. My grandmother's *leave him*
more poultice than curse. But I'm already dragging
what's left of him through the sliding glass door.

II.

Jungle gym, 1990

Through moon sheen and honeysuckle, *what's left,*
what's left? Over carpet, I'll pray that his knees
won't sugar and seethe. *Where does it carry us,*
saving what cannot be saved? I should give

myself to my playset's slide all night instead
of anger, should slink my thighs through monkey bars,
their still-warm steel flushing my skin as I slip
over dented bars and hang. I'll drag him

through dreams. This is history. A fury
of rust. I'll trust the galvanized pipes tonight,
the hurried concrete, the heat-scorched clay.

I'm not content to sway here, lost squall of girl,
so lapsed I'm nuclear. His dinner, what's left
of his legacy, has already been thrown to the dogs.

III.

Korsakoff's syndrome, Hibachi Grill, 2011

He's effigy, not legacy, a universe unhinged—
At his birthday lunch he's scarcely married to recall,
locking his chopsticks into a pot sticker's
pan-seared underbelly, scallions hanging

untethered from the gash. It's not the cicada
he slit esophagus to ganglion with his mother's nail
file because it was wings down in drain water,
and he wanted its hymn to unpetal in his hands,

for his fingers to gleam with plasma and throat call.
Later, his brain will echo the cicada's haunting
need, the song of a body thriving toward

heirloom, not harm—nymphal instar sloughing
its skin, eggs scarred into the womb of a tree.
He's palming the blur of china, its porcelain wail.

IV.

Flashback

Pity the china arcing toward the wall—
demoiselle cranes inked into silk, feathers
blushing with river froth. Suffer his brain
this furious chemical circuit. He tears his napkin

at the restaurant table. Slits of paper,
shards aligning, while my mother pays the bill.
I watch his muscle memory, the table constellating
under his grasp: Southern Cross, Ursa Major.

Then his flashback—air force sergeant, Aleutian
Islands, muscles mapping the crusade. His body
bright with another burning: memory traces,

not bay doors splayed in the fuselage. Oblivion,
bombs surging through longitude. His neurons
like oleanders stretching their petals through ash.

V.

1924–2011

His neurons are oleanders stretching their petals
through ash, *moving beneath him like the beginning
of the world*. So let's start with fringed corolla,
narrow lanceolate, downy seeds settling on the faces

of the dead. Let's start with his leather recliner,
the way I'm sheathing his blacked-out shoulders
in chenille, coiling my legs around him, his tangle
of oleander ferrying us both into night.

I don't know there's already a river seething,
impulsively riptide, within him, a river baptizing
him in dark water. I only know to purge

my lungs of the tree-scarred matrix of anger
and longing until it's singing I drown in, not his body.
I only know to dive until I'm new.

THE DAY HE BECAME AN AURORA BOREALIS

When I call about my grandfather's
cerebral atrophy, my mother won't say
he's heaving his dinner plate

against the wall again, won't tell me
he's on his knees, palms full of potatoes,
crushing their lukewarm opulence

into the kitchen rug. Even when
clouds intercept a swirling nexus,
an aura of plasma haunts the dark,

a forbidden spectral emission.
So when I call about his hippocampal
hemorrhage, I don't expect her

to say he's wearing a diaper low
on his hips, that he's bivouacking
himself in the carport, stripping

off sweatpants, pointing at the sky.
She'll say *he's fine*. She'll say *he's
the same*, only I'll hear that his

glial cells are turning into subvisual
red arcs. That his axons are breaching
the next solar tempest. I'll listen

for how they're pelting the vista:
hitch of static, plasma luminescence,
her voice going dead on the line.

THE MANDOLINE

When my grandfather writes
        in his will that my mother must
                witness his cremation, she'll stare
        as white cotton

and cardboard inter
        her father. She'll watch him
                enter the chamber headfirst.
        Because she's hungry,

or realizes his desire
        to be cruel to her, she'll imagine
                he's a gingerbread man, disciple
        of dough who,

when the timer expires,
        will thrust his body from the oven
                and run. Until he's removed and cooled,
        his wreckage milled

with a motorized blade
        and returned to her hands,
                she'll laugh his life into a harmless
        equilibrium—his life

like a stone irreverent
        to torque. Her rage
                like the silky skin of water. She'll laugh
        her way past the funeral home

director consoling my grandmother
        through insurance claims and death
                certificates, trusting she's finally mastered
        her father. But what is mastery

but another illusive
> dialectic, another rupturing of terms?
>> I'm six, enamored by parallel surfaces
> of cheap plastic,

by a brutal body
> entrusted to the kitchen armoire.
>> It perches with my grandfather's
> blush bone china,

albatross among a horde
> of enamel darlings. When he turns
>> his back, I'm urging a plum along
> its adjustable incline,

trusting the device to caress
> whatever it transforms. I don't know
>> that soon, I'll be watching threads
> of blood skirt my thumb

until he looks at me.
> I don't know that both of us standing
>> there in silence will begin to laugh,
> and that for years I'll lark

my way through every
> absurdity of pain until I learn
>> laughter is not passion, but denial's swift blur
> into languor. Like my mother,

I'll never master the thick
> moons abandoned on the mandoline's
>> blade—the ruins that gleam or my own body
> shamed—my blood

aroused by these plays
    of representation, my blood crying
        do not save love for things. Throw things
    to the flood.

II

THE END OF THE UNIFIED FIELD

> *what should I know*
> *to save you that I do not know . . . ?*
> —Jorie Graham, "The Dream of the Unified Field"

I.

Instead of winter, a cache of ashes, my grandfather
     threshed then yielded to air. I'll say *graupel*, when I mean
          I've spooned from his urn masqueraded with cloisonné blossoms.
               Hail, when I mean I've clutched *my inheritance* until
it has flown. Not tempest, but effigy exhaling.
     What's left of him seducing a swarm of super-
          cooled clouds, the love affair gone as it matrixes
               through gust. I watch him ease back into atomic
ordering. Sutures of bone interlacing in wind.
     His body confabulating like stars through a barrage
          of sky. I watch his body glitter the air
like quartz. I watch him rise through sun-stained fields
     of soybeans, deform the ether with his vector field,
          each fleck of him a *stippled star*.

II.

How long have I stood at this highway guardrail,

   watching his body repattern? He's crystal now,

      avalanche, a system deferred by conversion.

            How long have I watched his body rasp in the squall?

At skyline, he riots. I'm ensnared by his stroboscopic

   motion. I trace his dervishes through each illumination

      angle—tangent plane. Surface normal. I watch him,

         susurration in the sky's braille of snow.

He loiters in my gaze, radiant before he's swallowed

   again. The wind's turned his body to coordinates,

      a swarm that obeys the sun's scattered urges,

its streaks of chartreuse and coral. Is this what it means

   to taper into confluence, to haunt the spaces

      where the body, in ecstasy, threw open its wings?

III.

He's a man testing the limits of a field that never held
      him long—1983, Christmas tree,
           his blue satin bathrobe kitschy in the flash.
                Tinsel's fervent across a topography of fake
needles, candy canes splicing rouge against pale.
      Nothing interrupts the spray of ornaments
           but his eyes detained by the camera's tear of light.
                Later, he's lax across the sheet-strewn Chesterfield,
calico pillow slipped between his thighs.
      His coffee table's littered with Chardonnay glasses,
           a geometrical ashtray filled with half-smoldering butts.
Smoke roams the air. I don't want to know where his pants
      have gone, why my grandmother's snapping this mise-en-scène.
           These aphasias are only memories eliding. Open ellipses.

IV.

Memories, not collimated rays sharp in the flash.

      My grandfather in bathrobes, gingham sweaters, knot-softened

           ties caressing his neck. My grandfather in Speedos

                on the patio chaise where he suns with breakfast mimosas,

lazes like Ingres's *Grande Odalisque*,

      drunk past symmetry. Christmas 1987

           and he poses under my grandmother's quilt, aperture

                in motion, the day conceded to fingers of gin.

The last light blazes through half-open blinds,

      his face rashly chiaroscuro. I'm seven, and the limits

           of my world are dust pixelating in air that hazards

another threshold. Flash. Click.

      Light vignettes, cuts the scene to saturation.

           What is a photo stripped to its final exposure?

V.

Stripped by exposure, he dazzles in the haze—

    not man but calamity of hair, white underwear,

        a mute insurgence live-wiring me to his luminance.

            I have no words for the quilt that falls with his body,

the animal, serpentine, that rises with his breath.

    No words for why he's trusted with girls—

        sisters, nieces, the next ripe surge of daughters—

            why my aunt won't leave him alone with her son.

I don't know how long his blackout will vibrate

    across this room, the years, or how such scenes

        become the latticework of family recall.

I learned to carry the referent of my grandfather,

    not his wreckage. His invisible, latent image.

        To ask, was he body—*really body*—or negative?

VI.

His ashes, glossy as silver halide, lift
      toward a light that divulges: *effigy exhaling, sutures*
           of bone. As the wind takes over, I watch him disband
                  in a spectral valence until everything darkens, turns
infrared. He's a collage of signs enticing
      the next great signifier. Vanished words traipsing
           the boundaries of order, his dove-gray traces riveting
                the air. I dust off his relics in my palm's taut lines
that won't revive the sky or fields of soybeans,
      estrange a highway already clenched by ice.
           He's a flurry of encoding, a vector radiating—
referent, not wreckage. *Latent image.* Aphasia,
      not exposure, not the limits of his world: nothing
           remains of his final luminance. *Nothing remains.*

THE TRUTH OF THEM

Each spring: the Bradford
    pear tree's merciless aroma

        of sex. No matter the hardwood
    mulch trafficked

for pine straw
    or my grandmother's

        shearing, the smell pulses
    through the yard

like cats skulking
    the trenches of grass

        islands, rubbing their spare
    bodies against

sun-blissed bark.
    Fifty, testing positive

        for chlamydia, she believed
    the pearl stain

on her underwear
    was some vestige of her body

        refusing trespass. Grandmother's
    doctor asking,

Is there a chance your
    husband's been unfaithful?—

        As if faith had ever been
    the fabric swathing

her body to his body.
       As if infection came

              from a Holiday Inn toilet,
      his lie like semen-swill

staining the humid
       reach of air and pear

              flesh. And when she asks
      again, and he pitches

her cage of zebra
       finches down the stairs,

              the cage's door, like the truth
      of them, unhinges

its gravity lock:
       birds, mated for life,

              crash-landing into railing.
      Birds, jeweled

with contusions,
       accelerating with heat.

              After he's gone to bed,
      she'll turn to their map

of scat—tracks of creamy
       urate she'll trail as she calls

              to them, panic constellating
      the carpet. Because love

is not always vengeful,
        she'll wait all night for a single

            song. Years later, she'll read
somewhere that neurons fire

in similar patterns when
        a bird is singing or sleeping,

            an adaptation more primal
than sweet—*This need*

to make patterns,
    to build meaning

            when hope no longer consoles
us, is how we survive.

When she finds them
        in the kitchen curtains—

            shocks of feather nestled
into French cotton—

they're still breathing.
        Even hurt, their wings

            refuse not to touch. When hope
no longer consoles us,

we unhinge, we crash
    -land, we sing in our sleep.

            How else, after all, will we
master our mating song?

MY GRANDFATHER'S SUITS

With the air-conditioning's metrical gush
they're irrepressible, hainting and throating

like lost souls, but I'll suspend my belief
and call this a resurrection, one year gone

and he's a man hard up for heather-worsted
trousers, gabardine barrel-cuffed shirts.

A man who must loathe my hands on his
double-breasted jackets, the way I've creased

and stacked a haul for the Goodwill,
thumbed through his sharkskin vests. Perhaps

he's here for the letter I discovered in his stash
of ties while separating stripes from solid—

The Boys in Room 324 penciled across its face.
To finger its clasp and find a triptych

of Vitruvian gods. Imagine a god, knees bent
as if to hold a fallen world, as if to say

this is awakening. A second on top, bluntly
fucking his mouth, as if his chiseled body

is what remains of beauty. No words, just
flesh, third god shuddering inside the second

as though he were *Bulbophyllum nocturnum,*
the only discovered night blooming orchid.

Perhaps he's come to recoup his signature—
Love, K inked into the second god's ribs,

to secret away this relic in its hitch of vellum
like he's slipping it under a hotel door.

As though he's reliving the knock, a door's
fast metal. Bodies gyroscopic on Berber

carpet. To remember how it is to live for
the end of the world, a sun fevering under

gravity's visceral hold. To wake, one lover
tracing the folded letter over his stray

shawl lapel, pressing its creamy skein
into the jacket pocket stitched at heart level.

A resurrection, for his body to throng
again among his suits before they're gone

like his leather recliner trucked to the land
-fill, like his aftershave flung into black

trash bags. A return to life when living
was to tangle one's body up in orchid

blossoms, to ride their earthy musk into
a *beauty we are barely able to endure*.

THESE ARE NOT NICE BIRDS

Nay, I'll have a starling shall be taught to speak.
—Hotspur, Shakespeare's *Henry IV, Part 1*

The starlings ravaging the dish
meant for ferals are *darkinfested*,
their rasping calls hexing the air.

Yet the kibble they learn to jaw
transfixes me, their life-drive
miring the heat-flecked weeds

all June. When I discover a wing,
disembodied, in the garden I bend to
each morning, its flesh conspiring

with torn feather and noon fervor,
I don't think of the calico tom,
all ribs and slink, stretching

his haunches in the dust
like a bearded iris. I think of how my love
yokes his body to mine

until we are dusk-stained rhizomes
stunned into linen, our nodes of pleasure
perpendicular to the dark

earth encircling us. In 1890,
Eugene Schieffelin released sixty
European starlings in Central Park

so that every Shakespearean
bird could find sanctuary in the New World.
Before them, skylarks,

song thrushes, and nightingales
zigzagged across skies, dead
by first spring thaw. But the starlings

bred mercilessly, roosting in hordes,
feasting on everything they could
touch. Soon they swooned

from Alaska to Florida
with such intensity that in 1960
a throng would crash

into a Lockheed Electra,
crippling the engine with their bodies
over Boston. But history

is its own duplicity. I only
want to think of my love's thinly
muscled silhouette churning

in the last of the light
when he stands to dress, not cage doors
opening into a heartless New York spring.

I want to savor the image of him washing
my salt from his body
so his wife won't seize upon

the scent of another woman.
And when he's gone, I'll think only
of the wing I'm burying

among my irises, how
the starling it was hewn from
must have surged across the garden

in rhythmic tessellation,
the wind charting its heave and flood
like the last beautiful shame.

THROUGH A GLASS DARKLY

Photographs state the innocence, the vulnerability of lives heading toward their own destruction, and this link between photography and death haunts all photographs of people.
—Susan Sontag, *On Photography*

Before glaucoma forced him to surrender his license, my grandfather threw the key to his home office filing cabinet into a gulley off a state highway, idled until he saw it land in a patch of wild violets, and never looked back.

After his death and a locksmith, my mother cataloging papers to throw away or shred, she found a black leather journal bursting with his small, insistent cursive in the drawer stripped with masking tape, *miscellaneous* scrawled in obtrusive red letters. Behind it, twenty more journals shoved against metal and file folder, arranged by year.

When she struggled to disengage them, the drawer hinged toward her. Journals plunging to the carpet. Journals limp beside garbage bags stuffed with tax returns and expired depository receipts.

Every man keeps a journal, even if he never writes a word.

To find a journal is one thing—a moment of graphite, pencil's cruel liaison with paper. A moment of leather warming in my mother's hand.

To hold an artifact, another.

What she found—Polaroids glued on back leaves. Naked men posed over beds, their hard cocks stretched on their bellies like sunning garter snakes. Barely legals standing akimbo, underwear cupping their scrotums. Entries itemizing names, price paid in US dollars, dimensions of each organ limp and aroused. The positions in which he fucked them.

Another entry—*Happy birthday to me—40—I'm telling her—*.

But the pictures whisper their own rapt truths.

Seventeen, air force, World War II—how he sewed them into pocket linings of his uniform with a needle he'd hide in his shoe. When he decoupaged them, creased and torn at the joints of folding, how he must have trusted that pain was the proof of survival.

Twenty-seven, Korea, men dressed as UN Madams and Juicy Girls.

Bus depots, alleyways, tryst after tryst—city guys lacquered into tight pants. Junkies so skinny their cocks looked like pythons. Hard up goodtime boys.

I don't want to ask him, *why did you marry my grandmother?* I don't want to ask him, *what did it take for you to put yourself inside of her?*

Instead, I'm writing on the first blank page I can find, *you should have loved who you wanted.*

I'm writing, *to save you would have meant the end of both of us.*

LETTER TO MY GRANDFATHER, WHO LIVED TWO LIVES

Your pocket
of half-moon Chuckles
candy crushes

between summer's
hustle and your suit coat
as you dash

between Greyhound
and bus depot, a slurry of urine
and body odor

hailing its tang
like another nude hymnal,
a hallelujah

that grieves
with the heat—all body—
turning even

candy into ribbed
lines of luscious. The jelly
all grit and sweet

like a boy's
skinned knees, flecks
of mica

sheening from thick
sugar scabs only the most reckless
can reap by

the end of a hard
season. It hurts my teeth just
to look at that

row of pleasure
tethered in plastic you tear
with your fingers,

teach me to slip
between my lips and savor.
Love tastes

like cherry
stripped of its pulp and sour,
like licorice

dark and silk
as a man left—*O the rush*
before the wreck—

to sweeten,
then drag, what's left of his
body home.

TRUTHS ONLY STARLINGS WILL SPEAK

Wings rutting through dust like dazzling,
      hardened sky, I'm fool enough to believe
           this bird's dying, not sunning—body unfurling

like a gasoline stain, acrid iridescence rushing
      asphalt that could fry an egg to savory silk.

I drop to my knees as he arches and lashes,
      scapulars open as mantle feathers curl and lilt.
           He's a Japanese fan, throat tucked flush, tail

an untamed fractal spent as the heat striating
      him. What pleasure it must be to fantasize

one's way into the last murmuration, to be so
      aroused by the crush of convection to cede,
           then pant, then roil. What a child I am. Last

month, palms down over my lover's biopsy scar,
      I searched the melanoma like the heat of us

laying ourselves bare—costal grooves docile
      to the glut of keloid, lymph nodes feverous
           in their recursion. Bending to this rapture

his skin was closing over, I could feel his fear
      brackish as the lure of my touch. His body

a starling lifting under me, glitzing over
      a sky that hushes and frets into the last,
           unrelenting blue.

HOW TO PRAY

After Marie Howe

Start with one ear to the ventilation
grille to heed your father's saunter, a cadence
ending at your brother's bedroom door.

Hold his name on your tongue,
then whisper it through galvanized pipes
so that its raw silk grieving will

incite the bodies of G.I. Joes strewn
in his toy box, turn them to an army of saviors.
Let it turn the bicycle chain

lying on his closet floor into a Leviathan.
Listen for your father's soft cursing, the aborted
snarl of the family dog as its body

hits the floor. Listen for the cry
nesting in your brother's throat, the exhausted
animal sound only a wounded

body can make. Instead of weeping,
draw a map to the tree house you'll build
for him out of pallets and ropes

from the shed. Mark true
north on his Boy Scout compass in crayon.
Years later, at Christmas, buy baskets

of oranges and d'Anjou pears
that shine through twists of cellophane.
Wrap sprays of ribbon

glitzing at the crown, sign his name
to the card beginning *Dear Mom and Dad*.
Hope that this opulence will fill

the son-shaped hole pulsing
in the living room. If you can beg his last
known address from his ex-wife,

write a letter beginning *Dear Brother*,
end with *I'm sorry*. Knowing this isn't good
enough, start over. Write the word

brother over and over until it means
love, until it means *save yourself*, until it means
beautiful enough to disappear.

FATHERS AND SONS

After Peter Paul Rubens's "Leda and the Swan"

A swan and woman gyre in orgy, jagged
strands of DNA. Her thighs twist, rawboned,
in his thunder of wings. This is a Baroque leitmotif:
woman seduced by divinity. Woman

undone by a god. The arches of her feet
seize. Her fear muscles her forward under
his neck's insistent heat. His head coups
in the sever between her breasts. Her nipples

harden. Her lips lash his serrated bill.
Is this the way my grandfather took my uncle—
blood in *the air*,
               another *broken wall?*
Did his own father enter his body like a bestial
burning? Was it *white rush, dark webs*
in *a sudden blow?* Rape is never this beautiful.

THE THINGS OF THE WORLD GO ON WITHOUT US

I.

No vigil will riot my grandfather's body,
        so I'm holding the May 1987
Rolling Stone cover I find shorn and spliced
        between sheaves of his tax returns—Jon Bon

Jovi, leather's conspiracy of pleasure
        sheltering his shoulders, ringed hands grappling
jags of zipper. He's shirtless, silver
        chains, hair banged and teased stiff. *Hot Throb:*

Bon Jovi, cobalt transversing the cover.
        What is desire but a sin of omission?
My grandfather's talismans—Bon Jovi,
        Billy Idol, bodies cloying in tight pants.

Adonises resurrected by manila. His death
        like their faces in my hands, aching past ether.

II.

I'm aching past ether, my face in my hands.
      Why do we abet our evolutions,

leaf through them in the dark? Rupture is not
      the same as rapture, or how I induce him:

gray moustache, *Wall Street Journal*, lips plush
      as he's reading the numbers—NASDAQ,

the Dow Jones Industrial, statistics
      hurtling toward me like moths into glass.

Not market shares, indices, but cadence
      of bodies crushed by a gossamer

too cruel to be soft. What do we name
      the martyrs shattering us into eulogy?

Locked office door, photos entombed in manila,
      the bodies we closet in the night?

III.

Exile and pleasure
                musk our eulogies
like lilies we deadhead
                in the dark of us.
What is the body
                but an autobiography of secrets—
pretty boys, anthems,
                their vibratos smelted

to surges of guitar?
                Watch them spiral
through bridges shredding
                their bodies electric:
it's beautiful. He never
                lived to watch
the years conspire
                against them—broken men

now, broken songs. I shouldn't
                hold what I know
in my hands like this,
                some panegyric of paper
he gave himself to,
                as if grief and longing
are not sparring
                consolations. How he comes

to me now, unrequited,
                beatific: *hush. This.*
The amnesty, no—
                the effigy, of paper.

IV.

What is amnesty but a failed resurrection?

  I recall his anger—a sea nettle

pulsing and flaring in the night-stained deep.

  Flushed and plastered, he'd tell my mother—*If someone*

  would hit her, she'd be a better girl. Top-shelf

non sequitur cascading from the office.

  He's regal in his wingback chair, bookshelves

jacketing the perimeter, mahogany

  rolltop staunch at the heart. What shapes do they

  take, the past's bevels and ruminations

  that never belong to us? I'm eight, filling

his martini glass with water, my lips

  hovering at the cusp. *Milky medusa*, I think,

inverted jellyfish. Radiating ghost-striped bell.

V.

There is no ghosting, just opening one's mouth

to the ether. There is no vigil, just walking

into what's luminous and remaining

there. Bon Jovi, Billy Idol, or what

I haven't said—pulp erotica secreted

into Keynesian texts and *Time* magazine,

names like *Midtown Queen, Summer in Sodom.*

A cluster of skin mags creased and spent.

Wrecked origami. Cocks at gauche angles.

Men on all fours, every hole abided—

budding iris, tongued pomegranate—a collage

of men inviting me, as if saying:

Until trespass is beauty, the body

does not end. Suffer us its recklessness.

VI.

I'll suffer the trespass—my body, his body.
      Summon it until we both are reckless—

sweetest Gale, sorest storm. I'm on my knees now.
      Dossiers, cutouts, a plaque with his monogram—

Honorary Federal Bureaucrat.
      A joke, not my hands on his shame.

I'm holding what I can hold. If shame
      would abash us, if the storm would stagger us.

Highball glasses constellate the closet
      mantle, lime rind helixing from each rim.

If shame would abash us, would we still kneel
      at its altar? Let's latch the door now.

Let's sink into leather. Tell me—could we
      temper shame's frantic translucence and live?

VII.

If I could lie my way out of his life
    broken open, would shame still abash us,
would he carry it like this into dusk—
    covers glittered with perspiration,

photos lashing him to *the tune without words*?
    Glossies shining with slick florescence,
not the hard young beauties he'd rather hold
    between his knees. When we palm these

overtures in the dark, hold them to our chests,
    sigh like rutting does, what are they giving us
back but ourselves? As if to say: Lay me
    limerent. Lay me blessed projection.

Lay your hands on me. But we're already
    moaning—*just lay me down.*

TRUE NORTH, A RETROSPECTIVE

Don't leave me
alone to my ruddy din
of revelation——no——

to live is not
to remain luminous,
light a broken

jukebox,
the moon a thin-hipped
stranger slow

-dancing me
into his hard-spun radiance
all night.

Don't leave me
where light slicks the throats
of trees,

where my body
is just another smoke-stung
dirge of survival.

In this heaven
of all lines converging,
hold me

awhile, spin me
another lost song of longitude.
The moon

is only a half
-drunk lover who, lured
by orbit or his

own sultry shine,
is already calling me
home.

"Camera Lucida": "The discreet / side of revelation" is a phrase my uncle once said to me: "I am on the discreet side of revelation."

"Song": The line *"acutest at its vanishing"* originates from Wallace Stevens's poem "The Idea of Order at Key West." Also, the lines "The song of her feet / all grime and spent sneakers / kicking up hallelujahs" allude to Tracy Chapman's song "Say Hallelujah," especially the lyrics "Say Hallelujah / Throw up your hands / The bucket is kicked / The body is gone."

"Baptize Him in Dark Water": The line *"Where does it carry us ... ?"* comes from the seventh section of David Wojahn's "White Lanterns." The lines *"moving beneath him like the beginning / of the world"* refer to the following lines from Carolyn Forché's "Expatriate": "moving beneath you / like the beginning of the world."

"The Mandoline": This poem calls on (and appropriates language from) Lorine Niedecker's poem "Paean to Place": "O my floating life / Do not save love / for things / Throw *things* / to the flood."

"The End of the Unified Field": This poem is a sonnet sequence written in conversation with Jorie Graham's "The Dream of the Unified Field." It seeks to dispel the unified field theory of particle physics taken up in the original poem by directing its focal relevance to image and the degradation of both body and memory. The sequence borrows language and rhetorical architecture from Graham. My poem's commentary on photography utilizes language from Roland Barthes's *Camera Lucida*. Parts of the sequence also use language from Mary Oliver's poem "Starlings in Winter," especially her reference to the birds having "stars in their black feathers" and how they "float like one stippled star / that opens."

"The Truth of Them": The lines *This need / to make patterns, / to build meaning / when hope no longer consoles / us* allude to section 5 of Chris Abani's poem "Om": "I know this hunger, this need / to make patterns, to build meaning / from detritus." The scientific reference to zebra finches engaging the same neural activity when singing and sleeping directly appropriates information gleaned from Amanda Onion's article "Birds Practice Singing in Sleep" (abcnews.go.com): "[Daniel] Margoliash and the lead author, Amish Dave, a medical student at the University of

Illinois, found that the brain cells of zebra finches fire in very similar patterns while the birds are sleeping and while they are singing. And there may be a reason why the zebra finches sing in their dreams—to help them remember their songs. Songs are critical for birds in attracting mates and marking territory."

"My Grandfather's Suits": The end of this poem calls on Rainer Maria Rilke's first of *The Duino Elegies*: "For beauty is nothing / but the beginning of terror which we are barely able to endure, / and it amazes us so, because it serenely / disdains to destroy us. Every angel is terrible."

"These Are Not Nice Birds": The poet Lorine Niedecker once described her mother, a sufferer of depression, as "tall, tormented, darkinfested." Additionally, Leonard Cohen's song "Banjo" makes reference to "a broken banjo bobbing / On the dark infested sea."

"Letter to My Grandfather, Who Lives Two Lives": The lines "a hallelujah / that grieves / with the heat—all body— / turning even / candy into ribbed / lines of luscious" allude to Lynda Hull's poem "Chiffon," particularly the lines "Fever, down-right dirty sweat / of a heat-wave in May turning everyone / pure body." Chuckles candy refers to old-time sugar-coated jelly candies that come in flavors such as cherry, lemon, licorice, and orange; it was first produced in 1921 by Fred W. Amend. The lines "*O the rush / before the wreck—*" come from Kevin Young's poem "Cadillac Moon."

"How to Pray": The phrase "raw silk grieving" owes its origin to images from Brigit Pegeen Kelly's poem "Arguments of Everlasting": "The leaves are heavy / with silken grieving: soft packages / of sorrow."

"Fathers and Sons": This poem is written in conversation with William Butler Yeats's poem "Leda and the Swan" and borrows language from the poem's text.

"The Things of the World Go on without Us": This crown of sonnets engages with language and ideas from Mark Doty's *Still Life with Oysters and Lemon*, the work of Walt Whitman, and Emily Dickinson's poem "'Hope' is the thing with feathers—(314)." The form of the fractured sonnet is in conversation with Tarfia Faizullah's crown titled "Reading Celan at the Liberation War Museum." The phrase "*Lay your hands on me*" comes from Bon Jovi's song of the same title.

ACKNOWLEDGMENTS

My deepest gratitude goes to the following journals and anthologies in which these poems first appeared, were reprinted, or are forthcoming:

Adroit Journal: "For My Uncle, Who Learned to Fly"
Blood Lotus: "Rain Elegy" (originally published as "Apple Blossom, Dementia, Dead Bird")
Blue Lyra Review: "Rites of Passage: A Conditional" (originally published as "Cutting It Down")
Cider Press Review: "Baptize Him in Dark Water" (originally published as "The Body Worn Open, Whorling in Ceremony"); "Camera Lucida"; "Concordance for My Grandfather's Dementia"
Cincinnati Review: "Drunk Again, He Pushes Her"
Connotation Press: "For My Sister, Miscarried"; "Marilyn"; "Through a Glass Darkly" (originally published as "My Grandfather's Photographs")
Crazyhorse: "How I Learned I Had the Shine"; "My Life in Men"
Festival Writer: "The Art of Drowning" (originally published as "The Art of Drowning, the Art of War"); "Other Planets, Other Stars"
JMWW: "The Truth of Them"
Meridian: "These Are Not Nice Birds"
Nasty Women Poets (anthology): "Other Planets, Other Stars"
New South: "Song" (originally published as "A Story of Light")
North Dakota Quarterly: "The Day He Became an Aurora Borealis"
Passages North: "My Grandfather's Suits" (originally published as "Requiem for My Grandfather's Suits")
Quarterly West: "The Things of the World Go on without Us"
RHINO: "The Mandoline"
The Sonnets (anthology): "The Things of the World Go on without Us"
THRUSH Poetry Journal: "Truths Only Starlings Will Speak"
Whiskey Island: "How to Pray"
Witness: "The End of the Unified Field"; "Fathers and Sons"; "First Murmuration"

"Concordance for My Grandfather's Dementia" was reprinted in *Best of Volume 16*, edited by Caron Andregg and Ruth Foley (Cider Press Review, 2015).

"How I Learned I Had the Shine" won the 2015 *Crazyhorse* Lynda Hull Memorial Poetry Prize, selected by Alberto Ríos.

Many thanks to dancing girl press and Kristy Bowen for publishing the chapbook *Garden Effigies* (2015), in which several of these poems appeared.

I thank Adrian Matejka for selecting my manuscript as one of two winners of the 2017 Crab Orchard Series in Poetry Open Competition Award. I also thank Jon Tribble, Allison Joseph, and everyone at Southern Illinois University Press for their editorial direction and hard work.

For unyielding support—artistic, financial, and all manners in-between—I extend my gratitude to the Sundress Academy for the Arts, the *RHINO* Poetry Forum, the Woman Made Gallery, Yankton Federal Prison Camp, the Vachel Lindsay Home, my sisters in *Women Write Resistance*, the Visual Arts Center at the Washington Pavilion, Chad Christensen and everyone at Wayne State College, the University of South Dakota, and Stephen F. Austin State University.

Lee Ann Roripaugh, Natanya Pulley, John Dudley, and Molly Rozum—thank you so much for your exceptional mentorship while these poems were being written. Mark Sanders and Kimberly Verhines—thank you for everything.

Heartfelt appreciation goes to the many colleagues, friends, and kindred spirits who lent their eyes and hearts to me while I was writing (and revising) these poems, especially Staci Schoenfeld, David Levine, Jenny Yang Cropp, Holly Baker, Jen Ferguson, Teniesha Kessler, Marcella Remund, Heidi Czerwiec, Duncan Barlow, Laura Madeline Wiseman, Meg Tuite, Stephanie Marcellus, Darla Biel, Jim Reese, and Michelle Rogge Gannon. I am particularly beholden to Ruth Foley, Erin Elizabeth Smith, and Christine Butterworth-McDermott—your crucial perspective helped this manuscript in so many ways.

Jenn Blair, Jeremy Fajman, Simon Ostiadel, and Jim Owen—thank you for your faith and ultimate wisdom.

Finally, I thank my family, especially my mother, Debra (1954–2016), without whom my life and this book would not exist, and my husband, Matthew, for being my sweetest love and my truest north.